Aurora Uteralis

poems by

Katie Mihalek

Finishing Line Press
Georgetown, Kentucky

Aurora Uteralis

for Albert

ACKNOWLEDGMENTS

Thank you to the editors of the following publications, in which these poems
first appeared.

Beyond Words: "Aurora Uteralis"
Frontier: "A Body is a Body is Anybody"
Lyrical Somerville: "Rules of Design"
Mistake House Magazine: "You always liked my curves."
Spectrum: "Jonah"
The Underground: "all my plants are dead"

Thank you to everyone on the Finishing Line Press team for giving this
chapbook a home. Thanks also to Rajiv Mohabir and Daniel Tobin for your
kind words and mentorship.

To my family, my friends, my community: thank you for your support
always. Thank you to Ben Zackin, who has given me love and strength to
dive into these poems. To Abigail Ralph, for telling me this was a good idea.

Special thanks to Mikaela Fitzpatrick, Graeme Guttmann, Elisabeth
Graham, Kiran Maharaj, and all who have helped me workshop and pour
over these poems.

Publisher: Leah Huete de Maines
Editor: Christen Kincaid
Cover Art: *Sunset Inverted* by Katie Mihalek
Author Photo: Katie Mihalek
Cover Design: Elizabeth Maines McCleavy

Order online: www.finishinglinepress.com
also available on amazon.com

Author inquiries and mail orders:
Finishing Line Press
PO Box 1626
Georgetown, Kentucky 40324
USA

Contents

Mother

when the sauce is done, ready to pour
I recite in my grandmas' voices
drag a wooden spoon across the pan
if it has thickened

there will be a ribbon
shining white and clean.
now it is ready,
before it all runs back together.

look over the cracked cliff edge
you were never supposed to know these depths
cracked fingers seep over splinters
in the sky, light leaves water walls

trembling. My voice splits,
into the crevice, turns back to me—
ocean falls, soaks sea floor below
as it all runs back together.

sides cling together, reach out to each other
oh child, we must stitch back what they split apart
peek out from forest tangled tapestry,
little greens creep over dead stone divider

a fraction of the rumble, roots reclaim the path
I stand on broken road of reflected fold—I say,
why do I feel so small in such thundering silence?
it all runs back together.

Moses

when the sauce is done, ready to pour
look over the cracked cliff edge
sides cling together, reach out to each other
I recite in my grandmas' voices

you were never supposed to know these depths
oh child, we must stitch back what they split apart
drag a wooden spoon across the pan
cracked fingers seep over splinters

peek out from forest tangled tapestry,
if it has thickened
in the sky, light leaves water walls
little greens creep over dead stone divider

there will be a ribbon
trembling. My voice splits,
a fraction of the rumble, roots reclaim the path
shining white and clean.

into the crevice, turns back to me—
I stand on broken road of reflected fold—I say,
now it is ready,
ocean falls, soaks sea floor below

why do I feel so small in such thundering silence?
before it all runs back together.
as it all runs back together.
it all runs back together.

Topography

Things have been off
here, in my head,
quite honestly,
right now,
and before,
and soon after.

> Like my brain folds
> have been flipped
> and reexamined.

So I have to ask—
when you look
at a vine, a snake,
or a turning river,
do you see its thoughts?

> Because brains don't have
> eyes like a portal

to peer into—

> I mean a portal as in
> neuronal, not emotional,
> a portal to see my tissues,
> my pink and black and
> red.

And I want to spread out all those brain folds
Stretch out the *gyri*
sulci
See the ridges
valleys

> Expand the kinks and feel the cracks, dig
> my fingers into
> rocks, roots, rest,
> dig my
> fingers into
> dirt, dark, flesh

dura   *mater*
arachnoid   *mater*
pia   *mater*

dig my fingers into
the topography lines, feel
what I   have taken
what I could make.
On a hike, as a kid,
I told my brother
                        those paths from phone lines
                        made scars in the land.
                        since then, I wonder if

my potentials
are carried by wires
or trees.

i

Wooden Memory

in the fold
of ridges crunched,
accordion hills
leading to oaks
stretched high

above cracked pavement
and meadows
that flood from
the river alongside
sweeping gardens

land like a shaken blanket
frozen and lined with
potato stone walls,
left alone and greeted
by newfound forest—

she grows up, up through
towns remodeled, abandoned
farmlands, ghosts of ancient
woods before her own curious
wonder—not emptiness, no,

maybe loss replaced, no,
maybe enigma erased,
maybe poking out of the
memory and asking, where
did all my people go

Clamshell

I hear a metal bite
into stone shell layers
and slice into seaweed coating
to crack a mouth closed shut.

Brown wrinkles adorn fingers
that shake with everything else
but are deft with a pipe
and a shucking knife.

I taste tobacco with salt
on my tongue.

The grooves in the clam shells
match the ones around
your eyes,
and I feel the salt breathe through

the air and my hair and I forget
that my small fingers
are slimy and muddy from digging
in between the wet flats, so

they run between my curls and the sand
crystallizes on my skin

in the sun. You lean on your rake,
squint up into the shell between thumb
and forefinger, held up against sky,
a self-made eclipse—

rays swell around you
dance in a circle on water
knee deep for you and
up to my waist

brackish path to ocean
crowned with sunlight ring

you punched through with that wrinkled clam,
leaving the scent of tobacco and salt
growing in the marsh roots.

Convulse

Remember the maple leaves?
     Take the shortcut
behind playground swings,
       slide through the branches'
screen, slip along the portal. Mind

the roots that press and crack
       concrete hills on our path.
I will peel this picture
       from my brain, will meet you
behind your eyes with leaves on fire

that see no ash—I can hold them in
       my palm for you. They are handprints,
veins stretching tip to stem, five points
       like fingers reaching
back to branch joints

broken, knobby
       arteries leaking sap, flowing
down under each small step. Trees layer
       over synapse edges,
sky cradles nets of wooden bridges,

I want to bring this back
       against the black.
You said: I am losing my mind and I
       said: Keep going or
it will never come—

It is raining on the path.
       Dark drips down ridged
bark rivulets, lightning strikes.
       I think of neurons splint-

-ering along their stems.

Asphalt

Things are quiet,
here, now,
but before they were
loud. The dusty lamp whispered,
the splintered chair spoke. Now—
the candle wick is white, a lighter
is askew—on its side, completely
filled.

This place is clean, shining,
fresh. I move through
the space and don't feel
it bend around me. I don't
feel layers collect. I miss
that knotty rope, the woven
colors, the sheer curtain that would
pass

through and fall into fingers,
collect memories, collect
wrinkles. What is it
to erase? What is it
to iron knots
flat?

Jonah

Sitting in the belly of a Target clothes rack,
my 5-year-old butt is perched on the metal
rod, trying to not roll the rickety wheels off
this skeleton spine that frames doors in every
direction, slotted between hangar ribs. I

remember thinking this clothing rack, filled
with discount summer tee shirts, thin fabric
draped in pastel layers I could knit
my hands into, that let my bare arms brush
against slipping sheets and ripple against
goosebump prickles—that this was a special place.

How often do you stand in the middle of
clothes? Not piled, not inside, but with them
flat, around you, with space intact. I was
in awe. Did it feel different, to be in between

layers? To filter into this inside built
by hangers swaying in this softness, built
by light shone through dye, adorned
by plastic iron-on decals; this as a secret
signage. I sat in that belly and thought about whales.

Their filtering teeth, no, not teeth, like willows
on a weeping tree, their branches and leaves swaying
sheets of cotton, polyester, nylon. I was
swallowed into stomach, felt that underwater cradle. Sat
in that chapel cavern, organ ridges arched
in digestive beams, knit together because

this is what worship looks like, because
unlike Jonah, this is where I am
at home, to be in the middle of this layering:
so I sat, with the metal pole down the middle,
skeleton spine for all this swaying, down in the center

of that stomach

ii

all my plants are dead

my basil is the most dramatic. it rivals
the most theatrical actor,

collapses with the last drop, fainting
on the terra-cotta, helpless, how could

it go on in this dry desert.
my sweet potato vines are covetous.

more like curious, they stretch and reach
out to the iron bars, curl fingers up

and around the rust in a self-fulfilling
swirl, leaned so far over the pot

they might fall out. Look—

all my plants aren't actually dead, but
there is this hole in the soil of my aloe plant.

Listen—i call her albert,
i carried her from city to city,

and now she is the size of an engorged, i don't know,
an engorged aloe plant. She's tipping over

in her brand-new pot with 10 propagations,
her tips are starting to shrivel

because i haven't broke them off from their mother,
because i don't know, the whole thing is rather sad

when you think about it, and the whole thing gets
sadder while i'm thinking about it, if they are

choking off her roots—but i'm scared
to unearth her because there is a hole

in the soil of my aloe plant—
and what if it's a home for something?

(The Opposite of) Photosynthesis

Make note of when you write the best.
        Mine is in the middle

of the night: when I
just wake up from sleep, when my body is

told to pause and resuscitate, when I groan
        and grab

my phone that burns my eyes out.
        White fronts

        black, black, black
against eyeballs. Tendrils poke, unwrap

themselves and shake, grow from sides
        of my mind

and into that chasm, before plants grow
        towards the sun.

        I wonder what that means
for my vines to meet, in the center, when they reach

        towards
the dark. I am so tired—but look! Note down

at 4:52 AM:

        doors are a sphere,
        they filter through shade.

My eyes tear up. They cry
        from the blue light

before dawn.

Sage

I came home from quitting my job—there were cockroaches all over my counter and my sage plant was dead. Well, looked dead. On inspection, knees scrunched, eyes close to the cellulose, we squint at each other. Me with puffy eyes and it with rolled leaves. Don't touch it or it will crumble, that's how brittle it is without the blue, the H to O; it is paper. All curled up and dark, the white fuzz on the stalks—does it look like mold? No—

I want to kill all the cockroaches. My face is swollen with wet, and I stand in the middle of my closet kitchen, wooden spoon in hand, trying to catch their primal fear. I watch brown legs scuttle, frantic in being found out, back to their corners. The spoon slips. Antennas twitch back and forth, brown shells scatter sends little ghost feet up my arm, softly, loudly, close my eyes and deep inhale. I focus on emails and the sage plant. Neighbor would've took one look and tossed the pot, but she doesn't get as close to her stalks to see the fuzz.

Diagnosis: Stalks are still green.
Treatment: Give it more water. Focus on the emails. Send one to the landlord. Feel bad for the cockroaches because they're just trying to live their damn lives, too, you know, and massage the puff out of your eyelids and press send.

I glance over at the plant and see light through translucent green. Blink. Depuff. Leaves unroll and paper turns back to tree. They lighten, stiffen, resurrected. More water, more life, water turns back time. Or flips it. Getting younger or getting older? Filling up? Draining away, away from crossed paths and turn backs—I pull the knotted path and my string untangles to waves. It had always been moving along the curve—

I'm sweating

watching webs, watching
electrocardiograms, my heart formed
in purple signals, in lightning in the sky.
I feel the dome, the sphere in the atmo—
my head singes, my lips prick.

       In an electrocardiogram, people look
       for murmurs, palpitations,
       the skips and jumps

               where it disconnects.
the signal must travel
node to node through
muscle through muscle through wall.

       I throw the door open
       in this new house and I stand

close to the screen, let air sit
on the mesh and hot mix
with the freeze. I wonder how each water drop
conducts that arc, siphons
off static and lets the spark jump
       from drop to drop, node to node,
       skip down through sky and
       linger between humidity
       and diffuse. Lightning doesn't strike here,

it ripples, with this wall of water that
mists and breathes and I wonder again
what it is to stand on this conductor,
       what my heart is to hold the sky flash
       in its walls, pulsing over again,
       burning over again, broken muscle
       linked to light.

Rules of Design

My fingers push into my belly.
My little pouch springs back,
flexible, and there, two jagged lines
like surgical cuts in my pliable flesh.

I am contorted on the floor, cold tile
pressed into cellulite, neck strained
in butterfly fold, my back screaming
with tension: What is this?

I never asked to be a map of red
lines, red skin, flushed face. Who
gave permission for cracks to twist
skin into curves, point and say, look

at this growth, this rise and
fall, these waves that ripple, squish,
balloon. But they break their rules:
these marks are straight up over my stomach,

harsh, burning red, one, two, off center.
I look for a third, for a line of symmetry,
and am almost disappointed that I
don't burst at the seams.

Drama Class

I want to wear a blue feather boa
smoke clear bonfire dust through a paper roll
perch on a summit 4,000 ft above the ground on a mountain
with a tiara balanced in my curls. I want to wear those
skinny strappy heels I bought sophomore year of high school,
with faux silver leather and the little buckles. I want to wear
a chainmail link top that wasn't made to cover my wide set breasts,
that wasn't made to flatter my wide set shoulders, smudge eyeliner
on my eyelids and wear my black leggings so my thighs don't chafe.
I don't think the trees would care. I don't think the wolves would howl
any louder, the deer tread any softer, the spiders weave any webs
less delicate and reflective, the sun showing that single strand—
I want this to be normal. I want to do all of this and sit in the dirt,
stand on the stone and be as natural as the green and the gray for it.

iii

After the Hesitate

things have been silent
here for a while
the hush has filled the cracks in the plaster
and the splintered rails
tentative tendrils peek out and

around to talk to the flower dots
pushing
between boxes and planters
that aquarium framed
by walls of angled
seawater left out to dry
in the sun and the knife

strips away what was built
coaxes forward what will grow
little green seeds of algae and stalk
to settle—discover them holding hands
with terrace tile and a finger stretched
out in synchronous opposition
to touch an outside leaf—

You always liked my curves.

When I first learned
to dance (with a woman)
I forgot how to walk
(with a man)

Too tight
boots but I'm slipping
in my shoes.
Now I walk in a crater.
Drag black nail heads
and leather

into my heels,
try to fill this new
space with footsteps
and walk all over—
I'm feeling like my toes sink
and knees pop
to learn how to push my step forward—

I joke about my bursting
out but really
it drops down deep.
I hate being soft.

I'm mushy,
pliable,
flowy. I mean,
How do I explain
red wine stained on
dark lips?
On loving curves?
On my hips,
your hips, On black hair

mixed with red.

Music clenches a lathe
and shock stabs
with a feather.

I point to one corner
                    and then the other.
I don't want to drown, here,
on this glass-bottomed   street.

Aurora Uteralis

Peering down at slides of cells
packed in close, nuclei stained
purple and blood leeched pink,

my teacher told us that
vaginal fluid is plasma.

We all laughed, but she said
No, it's true, and vaginal fluid
was plasma. In the lining of

the uterus, blood filters past
its layers, cells stay back, solution
squeezes through, clear substance

emerges condensed and stripped,
filled.
            See, we are our blood.

Little curved pockets of red
floating along, oxygen carried from
vein to canal, from blush to bruise

from lung to air, plasma to planet.
Because see, when I first heard her
say our vaginas cradle that plasma,

I thought of stars. I thought
of gaseous galaxies
and burning serenity held

within my pelvis.

A Body is a Body is Anybody

Ask when, if ever, you will
become a woman.
Grow a tree branch, and break
off the buds. Build layers under
shell, feel them move
to the edge. Learn how
to pleasure yourself, come into
your body, hate your body, make
jokes on hating your body. Smile
when they tell you, you are
cute, not beautiful, laugh when
they call you, beautiful. Buy
a lot of dirt, pack it over
the plants, kill flies that
crawl on leaves,
leave them to burrow. Carry
your roots from city to city. Watch
the buds push out their petals, drop
away—you're still there. Come out
of your body; look into its eyes
and try not to run, say you want
to stay. Say you want to just be,
sit in that silence.
Stare at the sunset: it's cold
in the fall. You love it, how the leaves
tell time with color, before
they leave their stems.

What color is a chameleon?

Change comes in *fours*, here, in
this world of cells. It comes in *phores*,
here, in these layers:

One—the outer, holds yellow,
here are *xanthophores*, holds sunshine,
holds red in these *erythrophores*, draws stripes
colored outside the lines in a book
whose paper absorbs, protects, like skin

Two—the first iridescence
tucked underneath,
here are *iridophores*, holds crystals,
holds pigments that reflects waves
like ocean caps flashing as they rock

Three—the same as two. what is
something the same repeated?
what is feeling replaced, tension
erased, density shifted above to reflect
light as filtered color?

Four—*melanophores*. let it roll
around in your mouth, let it creep
extensions up to the top,
let it hold the bottom layer in
its connections, let it not fall apart
in the face of this movement.

I.

I said I could be everything.
I fanned my hands, my fingers shook.

tension stretched across joints
that can't take this reach, hungry,

light shone in skin between bones, bright.
spread out against sun that's hot,

let it all radiate into me, become me,
vibrate through my cells, reverberate

into two, four hands, press fingertips
to a portal mirror and let the images

flow through into underneath,
let the reflection vibrate my skin.

II.

Blue is close, Blue is hushed.
Blue is heads dipped in quiet
conversation, Blue is when I let
go and I see you.

Blue is short, Blue is small,
Blue is ocean caps flashed quick
and then they fall
up into a calm.

Red is big, Red is large,
Red expands and pushes
out, out, out, Red wakes up,
up, up, Red flashes farther

stretches bigger, spreads wider
with sun and flame. I cross
my fingers in perpendicular
and see through the grate,

shift my eye along the shadows
and watch the waves flash green
with my head thrown back and
smile, squeeze holes smaller and see

it mottle into brown. I can be
everything, I said through red,
I can be calm through blue
and energize through green.

Xantho, erythro
Irido, Irido
Melano, phore

I can blend myself.

III.

Are you blue? I ask,
turning purple.
She likes me red,

and the contraction stops,
fingers relax, stretch and ease.
I can be everything, if you want—

she likes me red,
and I savor that change
as it fades off my tongue

as I dip through the glass
refract through the mirror
rest my head on a shoulder

IV.

Did   you   know   that   chameleons
use their   colors to   communicate?
Did you know?
After all this time?   It's not camouflage,
but after   all this time, how do I   not make it
a disguise? How do I shift that density, let the   waves
          stretch   and release   tense
and condense.
Is my   skin a   rainbow or   TV static
                              mid channel change?
                              Because I say I can be

          EVERYTHING

but   what   am I   in this   *every*
                              I can't help but panic,
feel like I'm stuck
                              between channels,   but
I breathe and

          know that I am

every   thing   no   thing   one   thing   whole

Katie Mihalek is a writer whose poems have appeared in *Spectrum, Mistake House Magazine, Beyond Words,* and elsewhere. She is the author of the chapbook Aurora Uteralis at Finishing Line Press. She has earned a M.S. in Medical Sciences from Boston University and, most recently, an MFA in Creative Writing at Emerson College, where she served as Editor-in-Chief of *Redivider.* She lives in Somerville, Massachusetts.

www.ingramcontent.com/pod-product-compliance
Lightning Source LLC
Chambersburg PA
CBHW020223090426
42734CB00008B/1195